Table of Contents

Body Butter Massage Cream

Body butter massage cream is moisturizing cream with a thick buttery consistency. We use body butter to massage into skin of the arms, legs, and torso. It provides moisturizing effect. It can be quite sticky, oily, and greasy. We usually use at night before bedtime.

The most popular ingredients in body butters are Shea butter, fruit, and honey. These natural ingredients have their own properties like softer skin, moisturizing properties, antibacterial effects, and others. Some are confirmed by research and others through the observations of years of traditional use.

Benefits of Body Butter Massage Cream

Body butter massage cream will gives you a healthier skin. There are many benefits of body butter massage cream as follow:

- Reduce minor skin irritations
- Restore elasticity
- Helps even out the skin tone
- Provide sun and wind protection
- Relieve minor rashes and itchy skin
- Helps heal minor burns, sunburns, and cracked skin
- Absorbs into the skin rapidly leaving no greasy film

Body butter massage cream can make your skin healthy, soft, revitalized, refreshed, and taut. These creams are getting very popular and show the amazing results.

I have tried many body butter recipes and these top 30 homemade body butter recipes are my favorites. These recipes cover recipes for skin care and skin treatment in order to make your skin stay healthy and fresh all the time. Enjoy making these 30 recipes and choose your favorite!

Ingredients

14 g. of cocoa butter
22 g. of Hazelnut oil
14 ml. of water
4 g. of vegetable glycerin
14 g. of emulsifying wax
1 drop of Benzoin essential oil
2 drops of cocoa absolute

Instructions

1. Melt mixture of emulsifying wax, hazel-nut oil, and cocoa butter in a saucepan over mild heat.
2. As they melt, combine water and vegetable glycerin in a small cup.
3. Add cup of contents onto melted oils.
4. Heat as you stir vigorously.
5. Remove saucepan from heat. Whisk thoroughly as the mixtures cools until a thick, creamy lotion is formed.
6. Add essential oil as you continue whisking.
7. Pour into pump-top bottle and use on dry skin (this bottle enables the lotion to be hygienic and last much longer since you don't dip fingers into it during use).

Recipe # 2: WHIPPED BODY BUTTER RECIPE

Ingredients

1/2 cup of shea butter
1/2 cup of cocoa/mango butter
1/2 cup of coconut oil
1/2 cup of a light oil e.g. almond/jojoba/olive
15-25 drops of essential oils e.g. citrus/lavender for scenting (optional)

Instructions

1. Combine all (except essential oils) ingredients in a glass bowl.
2. Melt them in moderate heat.
3. Stir continuously during heating.
4. Cool mixture in fridge for about 45-60 minutes until hardening starts but remove while still soft.
5. Whip with hand mixer until fluffy.
6. Return to fridge for cooling for further 10-15 minutes to set.
7. Store in covered glass-jar and use as a regular lotion.
8. Keep at room temperature for best results.

Ingredients

4 tablespoons of grated beeswax
1 cup of shea butter
1/2 cup of sweet almond oil
1/2 cup of coconut oil

Instructions

1. Mix all ingredients (except almond oil) in glass bowl and melt.
2. Add almond oil and mix vigorously. Cool the mixture in a fridge until solid forms.
3. Remove from fridge and whip until smooth and creamy.
4. Store in a cool dry place and use as skin lotion within 3 months.

Ingredients

1 cup of cocoa/shea butter
3 tablespoons of sweet almond oil
1 teaspoon of vitamin E oil
1 teaspoon of sugar cookie scented vanilla essential oil

Instructions

1. Mildly melt cocoa/shea butter in glass bowl.
2. Cool for 10-15 minutes.
3. Add the oils. Mix thoroughly with hand mixer.
4. Put in fridge for a 15-20 minutes cooling until it solidifies.
5. Whip with hand mixer until butter consistency.
6. Store in a re-sealable container at room temperature and use as body skin butter within 6 months.

Recipe # 5: PEPPERMINT BODY BUTTER RECIPE

Ingredients

2-3 oz. of cocoa butter
6 oz. of coconut oil
3 tablespoons of peppermint essential oils
A colorant of your choice (I chose red)
Rubbing alcohol (optional)

Instructions

1. Use the alcohol to spray the storage container for sanitization.
2. Melt both coconut oil and cocoa butter in a double boiler.
3. Cool in fridge for 5-10 minutes until they appear slightly opaque.
4. Whip until the oils are creamy.
5. Refrigerate for 4-7 minutes then continue whipping.
6. Add the essential oils and whip until stiff peaks appear.
7. Put into 2 separate bowls and add red colorant into one.
8. Then use a spatula to add a layer of white body butter alternating with red until container is full. Use within 3 months of preparation.

Ingredients

1/2 cup of pre-prepared magnesium oil
1/4 cup of natural coconut oil
2 tablespoons of beeswax pastilles
3 tablespoons of shea butter

Instructions

1. On medium heat and in a quartz-size mason-jar, combine the beeswax, coconut oil, and shea butter and melt.
2. Remove from heat and cool to room temperature.
3. When slightly opaque, blend the mixture in a blender.
4. Slowly add magnesium oil while stirring continuously until well blended.
5. Refrigerate for 15-20 minutes and stir further to a nice consistency.
6. Store at room temperature and use on skin as normal lotion for up to 3 months.

Recipe # 7: COCOA MANGO WHIPPED BODY BUTTER RECIPE

Ingredients

1 cup of shea butter
1 cup of cocoa/mango butter
1/2 cup of coconut oil
1/2 cup of a light oil e.g. almond/jojoba/olive
20- 30 drops of essential oils like citrus/lavender for scenting

Instructions

1. Mix all ingredients, except the essential oils, in a glass bowl.
2. Heat them in moderate heat until they melt.
3. Stir continuously as you heat.
4. Refrigerate the mixture for about 50-60 minutes until hardening starts. Make sure to remove while the mixture is still soft.
5. Then whip with hand mixer until fluffy.
6. Put to the fridge again for cooling for further 10-15 minutes to set.
7. Store in a covered glass-jar and use as a regular lotion.
8. The body butter should be kept at room temperature for best results.

Recipe # 8: BANANA SCENTED BODY BUTTER RECIPE

Ingredients

2-3 oz. of cocoa butter
6 oz. of coconut oil
1 cup mashed banana
A colorant of your choice (I chose red)
Rubbing alcohol (optional)

Instructions

1. Use the alcohol to spray the storage container for sanitization.
2. Melt both coconut oil and cocoa butter in a double boiler.
3. Cool in fridge for 5-10 minutes until they appear slightly opaque.
4. Whip until the oils are creamy.
5. Refrigerate for 4-7 minutes then continue whipping.
6. Add the banana scent and whip until stiff peaks appear.
7. Put into 2 separate bowls and add red colorant into one. Then use a spatula to add a layer of white body butter alternating with red until container is full. Use within 3 months of preparation.

Recipe # 9: ORANGE CHOCOLATE WHIPPED BODY BUTTER

Ingredients

1/2 cup of coconut oil
1/2 cup of cocoa butter
25-45 drops of orange essential oil

Instructions

1. Gently melt cocoa butter and coconut oil in a sauce pan.
2. Transfer to bowl and add orange essential oil. Mix thoroughly.
3. Refrigerate for 5-10 minutes or until mixture partially solidifies.
4. Remove from fridge and whip vigorously until it is light and fluffy.
5. Use rubber spatula to transfer the butter to covered storage jar and store at room temperature for use in up to 4 months.

Ingredients

2 oz. of coconut oil

12 oz. of shea butter (could be mixed with cocoa butter)

5 o. of grapeseed/sweet almond/olive oil

3 tablespoons of butter cream fragrance or essential oil of your choice

2 vitamin E capsules (optional)

Instructions

1. Prepare an ice bath by filling a bowl with ice-cold water leaving space for smaller bowl to fit in.
2. Use a double boiler to melt the cocoa butter, shea butter, and coconut oil. Use only low or medium heat.
3. Add the fragrance and vitamin E capsules as you continuously stir.
4. When they have formed a nice mixture, cool to about room temperature.
5. Store in a cool dry place and use as body lotion for up to 3 months since preparation.

Recipe # 11: COCOA BUTTER ROSE HIPS BODY BUTTER RECIPE

Ingredients

1/2 cup of cocoa butter
1/2 cup of shea butter
1/3 cup of coconut oil
1/4 cup of almond oil
1/4 cup of olive oil
2 tablespoons of Rose hips
15-20 drops of Rose essential oils

Instructions

1. Using a double boiler or a pyrex glass measuring-cup, combine the coconut oil, the almond oil, and the olive oil.
2. Warm the mixture of the oils on low or medium heat until the whole mixture is melted into a thick liquid.
3. Add the Rose hips to the mixture of heated oils and keep heating on low or medium heat for about 15- 20 minutes.
4. Then remove from the heat and allow it to steep for 30 minutes to 1 hour.
5. When it has formed a nice blend which is somehow opaque in color, cool in fridge.
6. Store in a cool dry place and use as body butter for up to 2 months.

Ingredients

1/2 cup of solidified coconut oil
2 tablespoons of shea butter
2-3 drops of sweet almond oil
25-30 drops of orange essential oil

Instructions

1. Put shea butter, coconut oil, and sweet almond oil in a glass bowl and whip to mix.
2. Add essential oil.
3. Continue mixing until mixture becomes a fluffy body butter (Use rubber spatula to scrape down sides of the bowl).
4. Transfer the butter to a lidded glass-container and refrigerate for use on skin for up to 2 months after preparation.

Recipe # 13: MANGO CITRUS BODY BUTTER RECIPE

Ingredients

10 g. of bees/jojoba wax
25 g. of cocoa butter
30 g. of shea butter
25 g. of mango butter
1 teaspoon of almond oil
1 teaspoon of vitamin E
20-25 drops of citrus essential oil

Instructions

1. Melt beeswax mango-better and cocoa butter in a double boiler over medium heat. Cool slightly.
2. Add almond oil and vitamin E.
3. Heat until mixture is completely fluid.
4. Remove from heat. Add essential oils as you stir vigorously.
5. Pour into storage jars and leave to set. Store at room temperature and rub as skin lotion.

Recipe # 14: COCONUT VASELINE BODY BUTTER RECIPE

Ingredients

7-8 oz. of Vaseline cocoa butter petroleum jelly
8 fl.oz. of Aruba coconut body lotion
4 oz. of Studio-35 vitamin E cream

Instructions

1. Put all ingredients into a mixer and melt on medium heat.
2. Cool to room temperature and whip thoroughly into a nice blend.
3. Refrigerate for storage in mason jars. Enough for about 6-8 oz. jars.
4. You could also add a strip of washi-tape across the top.

Recipe # 15: WHITE CHOCOLATE PEPPERMINT BODY BUTTER

Ingredients

1/4 cup of cocoa butter
1/4 cup of virgin coconut oil
1/4 cup of avocado oil
1 teaspoon of red Raspberry seed oil
10-15 drops of peppermint essential oil

Instructions

1. In a saucepan over low/medium heat, melt a mixture of cocoa butter, avocado oil, and coconut oil as you whisk the oils to mix.
2. Remove from heat and cool for 3-5 minutes.
3. Add red Raspberry seed oil and move saucepan into fridge for cooling.
4. Let the liquid cool for 45-60 minutes until it begins to set up but still soft enough for whipping.
5. Remove from fridge and add peppermint essential oils. Whip until mixture is light and fluffy.
6. Store in lidded container at room temperature and apply on skin using clean hands.

Recipe # 16: LAVENDER VANILLA BODY BUTTER RECIPE

Ingredients

1/4 cup of mango-butter
1/4 cup of virgin/refined coconut oil
1/4 cup of avocado oil
1 teaspoon of red Raspberry seed oil
20-25 drops of vanilla essential oil
20 drops of lavender essential oil
5-10 drops of carrot-seed essential oil

Instructions

1. Melt mango-butter, avocado oil, and coconut oil in a saucepan over low heat. Whisk as you heat.
2. Remove from heating and cool to room temperature.
3. Add red Raspberry seed oil.
4. Move saucepan to fridge and cool for 30-45 minutes until liquid begins setting up.
5. Remove from fridge. Add essential oils and whip until emulsion is light and fluffy.
6. Keep in airtight container at room temperature and apply on skin with hygienic hands.

Recipe # 17: SWEET CITRUS VANILLA BODY BUTTER RECIPE

Ingredients

1/4 cup of kokum-butter
1/4 cup of coconut oil
1/8 cup of jojoba/avocado oil
1 teaspoon of red Raspberry seed oil
25-35 drops of vanilla essential oil
15 drops of sweet-orange essential oil
15 drops of tangerine essential oil
10 drops of lemon essential oil

Instructions

1. In a double boiler, melt mixture of coconut oil, kokum-butter and avocado oil. Whisk as they get heated.
2. Cool for 10-15 minutes, and then add red Raspberry seed oil.
3. Freeze until a soft liquid sets up.
4. Then add essential oils and whip into a light and fluffy mixture.
5. Store in cool dry place in covered container and use as body lotion for up to 2 months of preparation.
6. Apply after each bath for best results.

Recipe # 18: EUCALYPTUS MINT WHIPPED BODY BUTTER

Ingredients

1/2 cup of coconut oil
6 tablespoons of shea butter
6 tablespoons of cocoa butter
1 tablespoon of carrier oil
2 teaspoons of castor oil
8-10 drops of eucalyptus essential oil
3-5 drops of peppermint essential oil

Instructions

1. In a glass bowl over low heat, melt shea butter, coconut oil and cocoa butter.
2. Add carrier, castor, eucalyptus essential and peppermint essential oils and stir vigorously.
3. Place bowl in fridge until oils are thick, firm but soft.
4. Remove from fridge and whip until fluffy.
5. Transfer to sealed mason jars.
6. Ready for use as body lotion.

Recipe # 19: HONEY LEMON BODY BUTTER RECIPE

Ingredients

2 tablespoons of beeswax
1/2 cup grape seed oil
1 capsule vitamin E oil
2-4 tablespoons of distilled water
8-10 drops citrus lemon essential oil

Instructions

1. Melt mixture of grape-seed oil, vitamin E oil and beeswax in a pyrex bowl.
2. Beat the mixture with a hand mixer as you add water slowly until they turn oily/milky.
3. Add the lemon essential oils.
4. Let the lotion sit for 20min then whip again.
5. Store in sealed containers (preferably in a fridge) for use on skin as body butter.

Recipe # 20: PINEAPPLE FLAVOURED WHIPPED BODY BUTTER RECIPE

Ingredients

1/2 cup of pure pineapple juice
1/2 cup of shea butter
1/2 cup of cocoa/mango-butter
1/2 cup of coconut oil
1/2 cup of almond/olive/jojoba light oil
15-30 drops of essential oils for scenting (peppermint or citrus or lavender)

Instructions

1. Mix all ingredients (except essential oils) in a glass bowl and heat gently. Stir constantly.
2. Remove heating and cool in fridge until hardening starts.
3. When still soft enough, whip until it's fluffy. Add essential oils and more pineapple juice until your flavor.
4. Refrigerate again for 12-15 minutes. Whip again to a nice soft mixture.
5. Store in a sealed glass jar in fridge and use as a regular body lotion.

Recipe # 21: HOMEMADE D.I.Y ROSE BODY BUTTER

Ingredients

1 cup of sweet almond oil
2 tablespoons of shaved beeswax
1 cup of pure or Rose water
20-30 drops of Rose essential oil
10-15 drops of any other essential oil you like

Instructions

1. Gently heat a saucepan and add mixture of shaved beeswax and almond oil. Melt them on low heat. Remove from heat.
2. As you stir the mixture slowly but continuously, blend in the Rosewater.
3. Add essential oils and continue stirring until a thick emulsion is formed.
4. Refrigerate in sealed containers for use as normal body lotion (suitable for use up to 2 months after preparation).

Ingredients

A cinnamon stick
30 drops of cinnamon oil
100 g. of coconut oil
50 g. of cocoa butter
50 g. of shea butter

Instructions

1. Gently heat the shea and cocoa butters on low heat in a saucepan until melted.
2. Add coconut oil as you stir continuously.
3. Turn off heat and cool for 10min as you stir regularly to avoid fast setting (once every 30 seconds is okay).
4. On cooling, add cinnamon oil and whip until fluffy.
5. Add pieces of broken cinnamon stick into mixture and stir thoroughly.
6. Keep in an airtight container so as to avoid losing consistency and use as body skin butter.

Recipe # 23: WHIPPED COCONUT OIL COFFEE BODY BUTTER RECIPE

Ingredients

1 cup of coconut oil
1/2 cup of freshly brewed strong coffee
4 capsules vitamin E
2 tablespoons of lavender essential oils

Instructions

1. Whip hard coconut oil in a glass bowl until stiff picks form (you may alternate between whipping and refrigerating for best results).
2. Once a silky gloss is formed, add coffee (cover mixture with towel to avoid splashing).
3. Use high-speed mixer to whip for 3-5 minutes until a finely-blended mocha coffee-scented cream is formed.
4. Pour contents of vitamin E capsules into the cream and whip thoroughly for another 4-5 minutes.
5. Add essential oils and whip again to a nice cream.
6. Store in sealed glass jars in a fridge and use every time you bath.

Ingredients

Part A:

45 g. of ritamulse

17 g. of cetyl-alcohol

28 g. of mango butter

17 g. of argan oil

51 g. of apricot-kernel oil

28 g. of cocoa butter

11 g. of glycerine

28 g. of aloe-vera extracts

6 g. of allantoin

11 g. of dimethicone

Part B:

297 g. of boiling water

Part C:

5 g. of phyto-keratin

5 g. of geogard

Part D:

11 g. of dry-flo.

Instructions

1. Heat all ingredients of Part A in a large mixing bowl until all are melted.
2. Add Part B (boiling water) to the melted mixture as you heat and whisk rigorously.
3. When texture has turned to a pudding-like, creamy consistency, remove from heat and cool to 45 degrees or lower.
4. Add Part C ingredients and whisk thoroughly.
5. Sprinkle Part D (dry-flo) into the cream evenly and whisk until no clumps remain.
6. Use a hand mixer to whip to your desired consistency before storing

in a sealed container in a fridge for use as body lotion.

Ingredients

1/2 cup of organic cocoa butter
1/2 cup of organic mango/shea butter
1/2 cup of coconut oil
1/2 cup of jojoba/olive/almond oil
2-3 teaspoons of peppermint essential oils
2-3 tablespoons of pure cocoa/cacao powder
2 teaspoons of non-GMO vitamin E

Instructions

1. Fill a large bowl with ice and fit a smaller one inside to prepare an ice-bath.
2. Melt mango and cocoa butters over a low simmer.
3. Add coconut oil and melt the mixture. Remove from heat.
4. Separately mix 5 teaspoons of cocoa powder and jojoba/almond/olive oil vigorously.
5. Combine the 2 mixture and whip thoroughly before cooling for 10 minutes in ice-bath.
6. Remove mixture from ice-bath and whip until a thick stiff-peak forms.
7. Store in an airtight jar away from direct sunlight and use as body lotion for all skin types.

Ingredients

1 cup of coconut oil
1/2 cup of freshly brewed green tea
4-5 capsules vitamin E
2 tablespoons of lavender essential oils

Instructions

1. In a glass bowl, whip hard coconut oil until stiff picks form (you may alternate between whipping and refrigerating for best results).
2. When a silky gloss is formed, add green tea (cover mixture with towel to avoid splashing).
3. Use high-speed mixer to whip for 5-10 minutes until a finely-blended green tea scented cream forms.
4. Pour contents of vitamin E capsules into the cream and whip thoroughly for another 4-5min.
5. Add essential oils and whip again to a nice green tea scented cream.
6. Store in sealed glass jars in a fridge and apply on your baby's skin every time you bath it.

Ingredients

1/2 cup of organic COCOA BUTTER
1/2 cup of organic mango/shea butter
1/2 cup of coconut oil
1/2 cup of jojoba/olive/almond oil
2-3 teaspoons of peppermint essential oils
2-3 tablespoons of natural white arrowroot powder (or non-GMO starch)
2 teaspoons of non GMO vitamin E

Instructions

1. Prepare an ice-bath by filling a large bowl with ice and fitting a smaller bowl inside.
2. Heat mango and cocoa butters over a low simmer until they completely melt.
3. Add coconut oil and melt the mixture. Remove from heat.
4. Separately combine 4-5 teaspoons of white arrowroot powder and jojoba/almond/olive oil and mix vigorously using hand mixer.
5. Bring the 2 mixtures together in one large bowl and whip thoroughly. Then cool for 10min in the ice-bath.
6. Remove mixture from ice-bath and whip until a thick stiff-peak forms.
7. Keep in an airtight jar away from direct sunlight and use as body lotion for all skin types.

Recipe # 28: STRAWBERRY SCENTED WHIPPED BODY BUTTER

Ingredients

3-5 tablespoons of strawberry juice
3-5 tablespoons of natural beeswax
1 cup of shea butter
1/2 cup of almond oil
1/2 cup of coconut oil

Instructions

1. Combine all the ingredients (except almond oil) in a glass bowl and heat to melt.
2. Add almond oil and mix vigorously.
3. Cool the mixture in a fridge until solid forms.
4. Remove from fridge and whip until smooth and creamy.
5. Add the strawberry juice and whip again until a nice strawberry scented cream is formed.
6. Store in a cool dry place and use as skin lotion within 3 months.

Ingredients

2-3 ounces of cocoa butter
4-6 ounces of coconut oil
3 tablespoons of tallow mint essential oils
A colorant of your choice
Rubbing alcohol (optional)

Instructions

1. Rubbing alcohol is used to spray the inside of the storage container for sanitization.
2. Heat mixture of coconut oil and cocoa butter in double-boiler until melting. Cool in a fridge for 10min until a slightly opaque mixture appears.
3. Whip thoroughly until the oils turn creamy.
4. Refrigerate for up to 10 minutes. Remove and continue whipping.
5. Add tallow mint essential oils and whip until stiff peaks appear.
6. Add the colorant and whip to mix.
7. Store the butter in a sealed container and use for up to 2 months after preparation.

Recipe # 30: LEMON COCOA BUTTER WHIPPED BODY BUTTER

Ingredients

1/2 cup of coconut oil
1/2 cup of cocoa butter
25-45 drops of lemon essential oil
A colorant of your choice

Instructions

1. Melt cocoa butter and coconut oil in a sauce-pan over low/medium heat.
2. Transfer to a large bowl and add lemon essential oil. Mix thoroughly.
3. Refrigerate for 5-10 minutes or until mixture partially solidifies.
4. Remove from fridge and add the colorant. Whip vigorously until it is lightly fluffy.
5. Using a rubber spatula, transfer the butter to a sealable storage jar.
6. Store at room temperature for use in up to 3 months since preparation.